GHOST/HOME:
A Beginner's Guide to Being Haunted

GHOST/HOME
A Beginner's Guide to Being Haunted

an essay by **DENNIS JAMES SWEENEY**

Ricochet Editions

Published by Ricochet Editions
www.ricocheteditions.com
Copyright © 2020 by Dennis James Sweeney
All rights reserved
Ricochet Editions titles are distributed to the trade by
Small Press Distribution
Phone: (510) 524-1668
Library of Congress Cataloging-in-Publication Data
Names: Sweeney, Dennis James, author.
Title: Ghost/Home / Sweeney, Dennis James.
Description: First Edition. | Los Angeles, CA: Ricochet Editions, (2020)
Identifiers: LCCN 2019955850
ISBN 9781938900334
All quotations from Clarice Lispector translated into English by
Benjamin Moser and Magdalena Edwards.
Original cover image Anna Atkins, "Punctaria Iatifolia" cyanotype 1846
Cover and interior design by Diana Arterian
Printed in the United States of America
9 8 7 6 5 4 3 2 1
First edition
Ricochet Editions

TABLE OF CONTENTS

I – Getting to Know Your Ghost   1

II – Between Ghost and Home   11

III – What Is Left Out Is the Haunting   19

I — GETTING TO KNOW YOUR GHOST

Yes, yes..., in a surprised fatigue some thing was not being carried out, sliding like the wind and disappearing forever; a cold apprehension was making her shudder; the long and tense silence was uselessly sharpening her senses...

— CLARICE LISPECTOR, THE CHANDELIER

See Fig. 1. Because the Confederate soldier living *inside* my sister was a function of my sister growing up *inside* our house. The empath told her something horrible had taken place on the land where we grew up, and the soldier was just one casualty of it. According to him we had lived among ghosts; we slept in rooms that were as thick with them as with air. When she was a child, one of the ghosts split off and got in her. It followed her all the way to Los Angeles, where the empath finally identified the ghost as the cause of her anxiety.

He extracted the soldier from her. He said he saw black fog and bubbles emerge from her body, and when he had finished with the extraction her anxiety was gone. She asked him about my stomach problems. Your brother probably has a ghost living inside him too, he said.

At first I did not believe it. Since the beginning, I have refused to swallow my sickness. When the first doctor looked at my flattening growth chart and said the word Crohn's, neither my parents nor I listened to him. When the second doctor confirmed it,

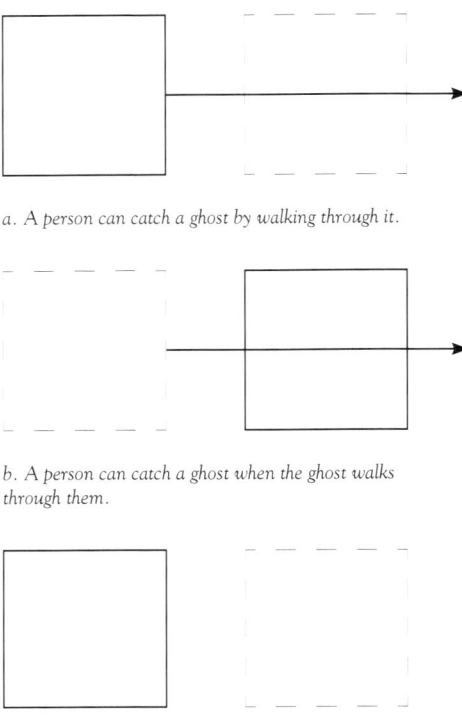

a. A person can catch a ghost by walking through it.

b. A person can catch a ghost when the ghost walks through them.

c. Or a ghost and a person can live side by side long enough that they simply unite.

Fig. 1. How to become inhabited by a ghost.

explaining that my immune system was attacking my digestion for reasons no one could understand, I believed I could fight the apparition. Millions of people had Crohn's. They accepted the ghost. I had been presented with it, but I would not take it into me.

It was true that the attic of our house, which served as a game room when my friends were over, gave me a nameless feeling when I entered it alone. Once during a sleepover, my friend and I heard a scratch in or through the walls and sprinted downstairs with our pillows. For the rest of the night we couldn't sleep. We called the source of the noise Marilyn Manson, because he was the only devil we knew of. Later I saw *The Ring* and woke up over and over in the night. If I had to go to the bathroom, I walked slowly down the hall to convince myself and any entities that I did not want to run. Walking back to my room, I imagined the worst: a pale girl with long wet hair waiting on my bed for me.

Nothing *happened*. It's not that the ghosts became visible, or that they observably terrorized. That was the exact ghostliness of them. Instead of haunting they did the work that science claimed it could make sense of: an overactive sympathetic nervous system, the body's attack on its own intestines. Crohn's is often attributed to the immune system's lack of exposure to pathogens earlier in life. My immune system never learned the difference between what is harmful and what is only an illusion of harm. Never mind the ghost that my father claimed, with hyperbole that approached complete seriousness, he saw drift past the doorway of our TV room. Never mind the name of the first owner of the house, which was, including her middle initial, identical to my sister's. See Fig. 2. The ghost's exact ghostliness is its resistance to stable narration. It gets inside the body and because it cannot be identified, it cannot come out.

Which left me, a decade later, still inhabited. After years of remission, my stomach problems had begun to come back. Maybe because I was waking to the profusion of forces that were not me,

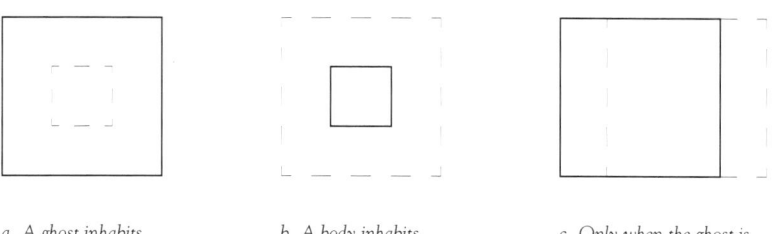

a. A ghost inhabits the body, but you cannot see what is and is not it.

b. A body inhabits the ghost. Because the ghost is everything, you still cannot see it.

c. Only when the ghost is part you and part not you does it become clear where the ghost begins and you end.

Fig. 2. Where a ghost lives, or is lived in.

those forces had woken too. The ghost was in the moodiness of my illness, in its sudden unpredictability. It was in the fact that the closer attention I paid to myself—the more I tried to solve my stomach—the more my ghost would react. It did not like to be looked at. It did not like to be known.

More than anything, the ghost was angry I had fallen in love with Thirii. For a decade, it had weathered what I called love with a smug eye-roll. People came and went and the ghost was never threatened; it had managed to convince me there would always be a ghost-shaped distance between them and me. But Thirii and I moved toward each other so decisively that the ghost became worried about what space would remain for it. The ghost expanded. It pressed at the underlayer of my skin. I could feel the ghost trying to convince me that I was it and sometimes I felt I was, to the extent that a ghost cannot heal but rather lives on a wound. It is easy to tell the ghostly feeling: You are troubled but you do not know what you are troubled by. You go against your best knowledge. Something in you wears your blood.

When Thirii and I began to talk about living with each other, the ghost redoubled its thrashing. It kicked at my membranes. I couldn't eat without the fear that I was feeding the ghost and not myself. When the ghost grew my stomach bloated, and I had to go to the bathroom over and over to let out the excess, but I knew the ghost was still in me no matter how much I let out. I didn't know it was a ghost, which was what made it a ghost. It had those dashed outlines. It was indistinguishable from me.

Then one night, the spring before we moved in together, Thirii kneeled over me and pressed her hand to my stomach. She drew out the bad using a Tibetan Buddhist technique called tonglen. It was dangerous, she had been warned, but her hand warmed me. She pulled the ghost out. The next day I was healed.

The next day she was as sick as I had been.

See, the ghost had discovered how to survive our love. It could travel out of me into her; after a few days, it traveled out of her back into me.

Fig. 3 does not cover the fact that extraction is far from permanent. We did not know the ghost could live on going-between.

But the signs grew like weeds in a sidewalk. The first apartment we tried to live in together repelled us as soon as we arrived. Not only was it uninhabitably allergenic, but a wasp flew in Thirii's face the second we opened the door. An unsayable presence resided there. It was not my ghost, but unsayability recognizes its kind. Thirii fell into a sneezing fit and we left the place, forever to hold our breaths when we drove past as if it were a cemetery.

After three nights in a hotel, we found a second apartment. It was clean of spirits, or we pretended it was. We saged every corner and chanted, "Cleanse, dismiss, dispel." We put plants on the windowsills and built an altar facing the window that faced the park.

Because we knew about the park. We knew it had been a cemetery until a century ago, when an unscrupulous contractor hired to exhume the bodies had dismembered corpses in order to make it seem as if there were more dead. He had gotten paid by the body. There were stories of metatarsals surfacing through the ocean of grass. There was also a story, one we told, of a man standing at the corner of the park staring at Thirii as we walked home one night. I didn't see him, but I told her and I told myself I didn't see him because I wasn't looking.

Then there was the story of whatever clung to us during a walk through the park after nightfall. In the middle of the grass a

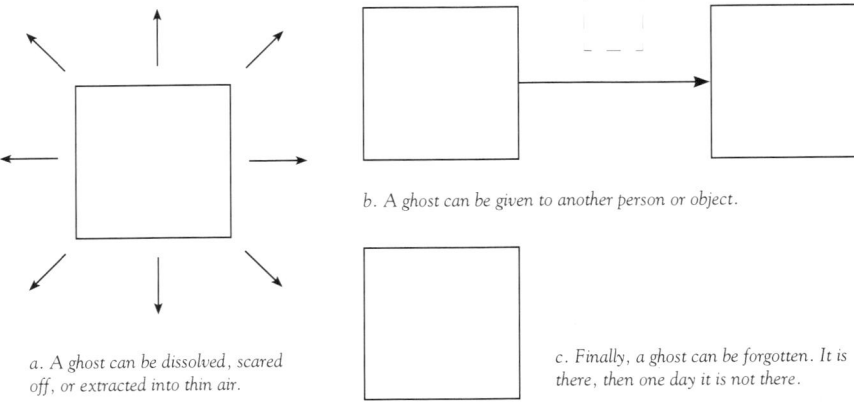

a. A ghost can be dissolved, scared off, or extracted into thin air.

b. A ghost can be given to another person or object.

c. Finally, a ghost can be forgotten. It is there, then one day it is not there.

Fig. 3. How to get rid of a ghost.

dog began to circle us. He barked ferociously. His owners ran after him helpless. "He never does this!" We kept walking. They fretted and murmured at the dog as we disappeared.

When we got back home we stood on the stoop before entering. What could we do to clean ourselves? We shivered at the encounter. Another dog walked by, stretched to the end of his leash. The dog looked straight through Thirii and barked.

1. Home is a place where your ghosts grow comfortable.

2. Home is a place you live inside as if you yourself are a ghost.

3. Home is a place you cannot extract or exorcise.

4. At home, you know the walls well enough to know they are living.

5. Sleep is only the waking of ghosts.

In the months that followed our move-in, too much that I won't name passed between us. The ghost had hooked its fingernails into our love and clung so tight we couldn't see what we flung at each other. At the same time my stomach got bad enough that some days I could not leave the house. The apartment crushed me into staying in it, even though leaving—the cool sun and autumn air—is what would have held the ghost at bay.

Finally I went to the doctor for my stomach. They had a camera with which they claimed to be able to see what I could not. They saw inflammation and said it was the problem. But I knew that inflammation was only a symptom, not the cause. They put me on a course of medication. The pills looked like circles, but who knew what was in them. They were sending in an army of ghosts.

6. Ghost and home share the same central vowel. An empty stomach, an empty dwelling, shaped like a pill. A place to get in but not to stay too long.

That winter, my parents were selling the house I grew up in—the house that the Confederate soldier had lived in before inhabiting my sister, and where I had acquired my own ghost. Thirii and I returned for a final Christmas. The bushes in the front yard were lit colorfully and the warmth of the holiday expelled every unknown. I ate ground beef and soft cheese and gluten-free cookies and Moose Munch and they passed through me with a peace that was almost haunting. My ghost was home. It left me while I was home with it.

Until a photographer came, hired by my sister, to record our last gathering in the house as a family. We posed on the porch and in the living room and in front of the Christmas tree before climbing the stairs to the attic, where we played pinball for the camera. Before returning downstairs, my sister had an idea: Stand in the unfinished part of the attic where the single unshaded light bulb buzzed, the room of the house where we had always been most afraid to go. No, my parents had told the buyers, they didn't know about any haunting, even though the buyers protested that ghosts would not at all deter them. We posed under the bare bulb, acting haunted. We were the only entities in the photograph, but we held our faces so straight that we looked like we were more than we were.

After Thirii left for home, my mom and I cleared the basement out. The buyers came in to check the wiring. They took a photograph of my grandpa's old chair. A fluorescent blur hovered above it. Look at this, they said. About haunting—are you sure?

When we returned to Denver in the first days of the new year Thirii and I began to understand the proportions of what lived between us. Either I felt good or she felt good. Some days I was house-bound. Some days her stomach haunted her. Her superstition related to trash after nightfall bore out. Angry, yelling, disturbed people gravitated to the dumpsters behind our apartment. The windows facing the dumpsters also faced the park. When I woke up in the middle of the night to pee I couldn't help but glance at the corner where those windows were, as if to make sure no one was standing there. To my sight no one was ever standing there, but to another part of me something was.

We began, too, to understand the city we lived in. Where no one believes in ghosts, there is no room for them. Hyper-rational joie de vivre is the newest technology for driving out ghosts and Denver is a hub of it insofar as the city is populated by an endless influx of people devoted to hiking and climbing and craft beer. No one comes for spirit. Spirit can't be named, so those who need names for everything do not seek it. In this way the nameless is crowded out. It looks for a home until it finds someone like us.

Go into the mountains. Start at the base, where land seems almost a default. Then climb, and as you climb notice the land's growing sureness of itself. The higher you get, the more the mountains seem to possess a deathless energy, resistant to interested ants like us. The trees are noble and the streams are thin but

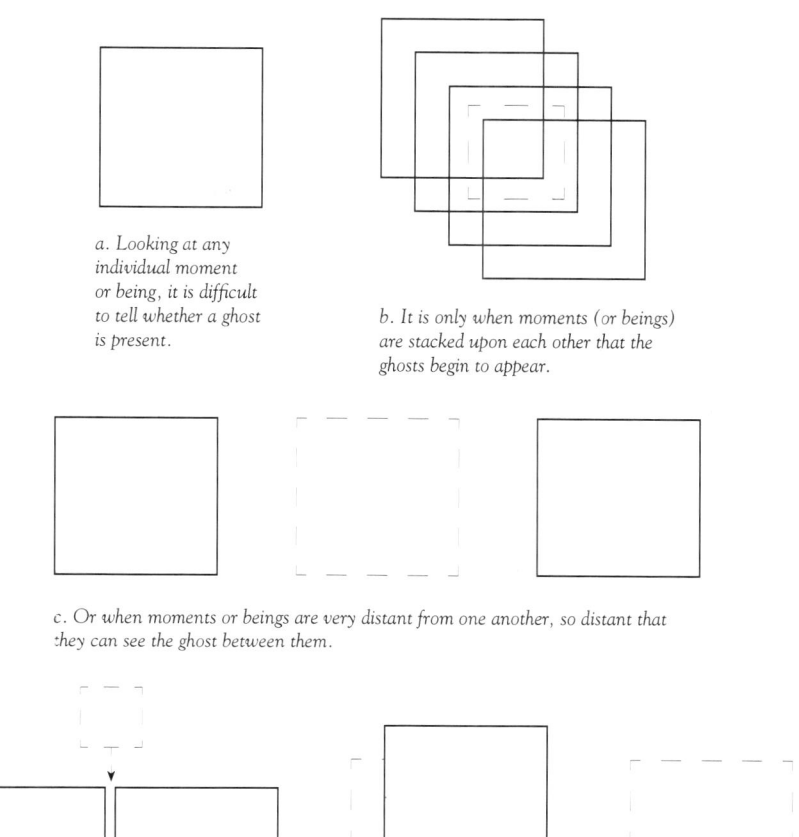

Fig. 4. How to see a ghost when you suspect or fear its presence.

necessary. Above timber line, both the sun and the mountains repel you. They do not speak because it is not necessary to speak.

But you speak. You describe the bleached stone like the whites of eyes. You describe the stiff bushes like fingers weathered thin and brown. Your feet tap on the path like a score, clearing it for our neverending flight.

And now you feel it. You are one of the circus of conquerors, born to grids and wires but hungry for the idea of the untouched.

You love the mountains because in them you can give the nameless a name.

7. You don't have to go far to find the ghost in you.

I promise: Living in my body feels like living in a ghost, or like a ghost living in me, and every meal I eat is nothing but ghostly because I don't know how much of it I'll absorb and how much of it will pass invisibly through me. My hunger disappears when I eat and reappears as soon as I've stopped eating in the form of fright. I am full but not full with what my body wants. I am full with the entity. The ghost keeps me strong enough to live in, but not strong enough to cast it out of myself.

Late that spring I returned to Cincinnati for the first time since Christmas. My parents had settled into their new house and left our old home behind. I wanted to see what my stomach felt like in a home that was not home yet; I wanted to understand what there was of me when I was somewhere my ghost did not yet recognize. The word "condominium" protects its hollow *o* with a cascade of locked-up syllables. It sounded like a solution and a healing.

I wanted to live in a home that was not haunted. I wanted not to be haunted myself. At the very least, I wanted to lose track of the haunting, but see Fig. 4. Life gets thicker. I wanted to go back while there was still something thin.

II — BETWEEN GHOST AND HOME

> *There were times when the room and the bodies leaning toward the plates, that silence that came from the fields, the atmosphere that no particular feeling could designate, was by her intensely understood— she'd stop short with her fork in the air, looking at them contrite and happy.*
>
> — CLARICE LISPECTOR, *THE CHANDELIER*

The new house was all the objects of the old house but rearranged. In the living room the dining room carpet sat under furniture collected from the front hall and the kitchen. The kitchen table sat on the rug from the front hall. The painting of my sister and me that had hung over an unvisited mantle now gazed upon the living room, and the glass console table beneath the painting held an uncomfortable distance between the couch and the wall. The rest of the room followed suit: Its objects held their breath trying to decide what to call this place that claimed to be their home.

Still, that first night, I slept without dreams. I walked downstairs in the morning as if I had always lived there. The stairs

In *The Chandelier*, Clarice Lispector follows a woman named Virgínia who grows up on a decaying country estate and leaves the estate for the city. After several years in the city, she returns home. Home feels both were solid and the patchwork living room cohered. Out the sliding glass doors on either side of the fireplace the wet concrete shone green-gray and the damp smell drifted into the house. In the kitchen, the fridge doors opened and closed with barely a pull. I blended my smoothie. I poured my mom a glass. My dad ate breakfast with the newspaper spread before him. The Reds had lost in an extra-innings breakdown. Dilbert's colleague, intent on inside information, followed him into a bathroom stall.

The house, I mean, was as clean as I had ever wanted. Below the main floor was a finished basement. No entities crawled along the floorboards. No spirits clung to the walls. The house was new but comfortable, easy without the vice of ease, knotless because its décor was practically random. Living in it felt like living an uninhabited life. The cut-off parts of the old home, just by sitting where they were, coalesced into a peaceful whole.

Later that night, I interviewed my mom. She said, before we had even started:

I don't believe in ghosts.

Really? I said. You don't?

I think ghost is the wrong word. I think maybe spirits is a more accurate—is that what you're talking about? People that have come before us that may live in a house or may live in a situation or

inevitable and impossible to return to; it holds the ghost of herself, of belonging, which Virginia discovers she both misses and has been fleeing from.

At the end of the novel, Virginia decides to leave for the city again. She boards the train with an inevitability equal to that of her return home. By now *she was feeling without comprehending that the place where one was happy is not the be in a—mostly probably in a house, I feel like they could attach themselves to houses more than anything. But I don't think of seeing ghosts, seeing a physical thing. I think maybe it's more a feeling of somebody that might have been there before.*

I don't know. I really don't think about it. I pretty much don't believe in it.

I asked my dad the same question. He said:

You really want to know the truth? No. Well, I've always talked like I did, because we had so much fun with it. Everybody got all excited. Everybody's arguing about it. But I never believed in it.

Yep. All made up.

I'm getting closer to when I die, and you've got to have some good information.

We laughed and laughed. But here is what my mom said about the house I grew up in:

If there's going to be a ghost in the house or a spirit in the house I think it would have been ours. I mean, it's just designed for that kind of creepy thing.

And here is what my dad said:

You have to have ghosts in a house like that.

On my second morning in Cincinnati, thousands of ghosts ran by the new house. The year before, I had been one of them. Last year's Flying Pig Marathon had marked the height of health and strength for me—a marathon PR, homecoming with the glow of victory.

place where one can live. She cannot live as a ghost.

Nor, however, can she live in flight from haunting. The end of *The Chandelier* replicates the end of *The Hour of the Star*, though *The Hour of the Star* was written thirty years later: as soon as she returns to the city, Virginia is hit by a car.

For her, neither state is livable. Virginia cannot inhabit home or her own rejection of home. And

But a week after I ran the race my stomach set in. The year that followed had undone me. So all I could do was walk to the end of the road with my parents and cheer for the ghosts of the old me. We yelled for the people who had their names on their shirts and for the people in pig hats. We yelled for the person in a shark suit and for Batman and for the people who were still smiling at mile twelve.

Every face wore the pain differently. Some set in determination. Some wore sadness. Some gave us a tired thumbs up. Some looked fresh, and some looked like they'd never make it. But I knew the face didn't matter. How much you suffer has nothing to do with how long you can stand your suffering.

I could have stood there forever but it was morning, and morning meant my stomach roiled unpredictably. As long as we cheered my stomach pressed at me, and before the five-hour pace group passed I was overwhelmed by the need to go. I said I would only be a minute, but my parents were ready to return to the house. They walked behind me while I jogged down the sidewalk with that old stiff urgency. I made it to the bathroom as barely as ever. I was surprised at what came out of me. It was less rotten than in weeks. Less blood. More well-being. Something had made the right thing happen inside of me.

so the ghostly ending arises, inhabiting Lispector's work in a double reflection: *The Chandelier* (translated into English 26 years after *The Hour of the Star*) echoes Lispector's last, more famous novel, despite the fact that the echo was written long before the scene it echoes from.

The Chandelier's sentences are both a labor and a revelation. Reading them feels like living in

That is the surprise of health: Sometimes, for reasons I cannot understand, my ghost allows me. Maybe it was the admiration I felt for the passing faces. Maybe it was the blood of my hand clapping against my other hand. Did the blood flow into my stomach? Did the cool air convince me I was alive? Maybe my ghost recognized the thousands of ghosts we cheered for. They were ghosts because I had once been among them. Now I wasn't. I was a frame for the living memory.

But a ghost never settles. For the rest of the day I felt good, or optimistic, or at the very least fooled. I fell into researching my newest theory, now convinced that it was true: "crohn's and living at high altitude," "can men be iron deficient," "how to increase hemoglobin crohn's." My third morning in the new house I shit red into the toilet. The house blurred, fell out of distinctness. Its comforting forms and lines became as pale as air. That morning, like the previous morning, I let my hunger grow. But I began to understand I was not fasting, with all its sharp pleasure. I was starving myself.

Listen: The ghost doesn't want to be called ghost. It doesn't want to be called at all. It wants to live in the muntins, the outlets, the hinges, the white between the floral curls on the couch and matching ottoman. When my parents say they have never believed in ghosts they mean a house you know better than you know yourself, while at the same time you cannot breathe inside it. Virginia's return home is the process of becoming old: She walks downstairs for breakfast. *With horror she had already lived her life.* For Lispector, 23 years old when she finished the novel, aging is as good as dying. She returns to the city to give up her ghost.

But what if we do not

they feel energies too familiar to be named. Ghosts are so immanent that they need no designation. I am already a ghost when I visit. I am the appearance of a memory, manifest for an instant but most of the time only haunting.

I live in the narrow vents. The underside of a lamp shade. The decorative corners of the dresser top. In plain sight, even: I live in the painting of my sister and me, where the starched sleeves of my button-up chafe my bone-thin wrists.

In the end, I cannot speak of what does not exist. To make a mountain out of invisible longing, or invisible memory, is only an escape from making a home. Home forms in lines and certainties, not in gaps. There are no ghosts unless we allow them. Then they turn around and live in us. Or, with stubbornness and a little Midwestern looking-the-other-way, we can refuse their influence. We can refuse to be inhabited.

And so I do not blame anyone for the ghost that is in me. I do not even begrudge the home that hosted it. The walls had that unnameable quality only because I myself had not found certainty. I was young and accepted everything into me.

Like my sister in Los Angeles, I looked for my ghost. Now I have given it this hollow, mouth-puckering name.

have to give our ghosts up? What if getting old means living with the feeling? What if, the more I am haunted, the better I understand that I must live alongside what I cannot contain of myself? Maybe it is possible to do more than run from or return home, to do more than reject sickness as a faulty premise. Maybe making a home means inviting the ghosts in. What does it look

I left Cincinnati after another good morning, when I produced a perfectly formed bowel movement, and another bad morning, when I shit bright red blood. My stomach had gotten better at the new house but not with anything resembling consistency. When I left, the walls felt suddenly angry. Or I did. Maybe leaving is the first touch of a ghost.

I arrived back to a cold and gloomy Denver. Rain coated the windows of the plane as it touched down. Our apartment was as exposed as ever to the energies that surrounded it, but at the same time I felt I had brought something back. I kept some armor, some awareness of myself as an unwilling host.

I knew return would be this way—both inhabited and inhabited differently. In that vein, I intended to finish with an image I wrote before I left. I wrote it knowing there would be no home to end in, given certainty's endless flight. What I wrote straddled the line between credulity and eye-rolls, between ghost as literal and as metaphorical rendering. It accommodated those who believe and those who trust only proof.

Before I left, there had been something I saw in the shower. It looked like me or what lived in me, and it gave you the chance to decide. What I saw could have been anything, or it could have been nothing more than myself.

like to build a life that treasures our unknowns?

I live inside the home of my body. The walls of it are filled with a ghost. But I will not hurry to death. Where Virginia is driven away by the spirit—*She looked at them and was now feeling united with them, knowing how to love them—so strong was the spirit of the house*—I will not let the spirit drive me out. The love is frightening to me too. It

Here is what I wrote:

Sometimes I am standing in the shower and out of the corner of my eye I see the white shower curtain fluttering in and out like a lung, as if there is an unknown force on the other side of the curtain humming with energy. Then I look down and see the water running out of the showerhead down my body and off my elbow, where it leaps toward the curtain. My fright rearranges itself. It is the water, and it is me, that make the curtain flare as if it has a life in it.

comes with no name. It pre-exists us, hollow.

But it also is a breath. It is a home inside a home. You can get inside. You can feel it. You are never alone.

III — WHAT IS LEFT OUT IS THE HAUNTING

How she'd passed through whatever could be without managing to touch it...

— CLARICE LISPECTOR, *THE CHANDELIER*

But I cannot end with that foregone conclusion. My grandmother haunts these words, precisely because of the fact that I did not include her in them. She was the real reason I went back to Cincinnati. She was living, no one knew for how long, the end of her life. I was going to write about the slow loss of her and call it ghostly, but that tack felt unholy. I couldn't do that to my grandma.

Still, every day that I stayed in my parents' new home I drove to my grandma's apartment complex and sat on the floor at the foot of her easy chair. We looked at photographs. She talked about how lucky she had been. There was a pathway between us that had been growing ever since I realized that love traveled two ways. I couldn't write about it, because my grandma was not material for an essay. But I have to write this.

Just before I left she and I were alone, talking in her living room. As if it were no surprise at all, she told me she had had a dream the night before. Grandpa was in it. He died ten years ago, but in her dream he stood visibly beside her. Did he say anything? I asked my grandma. I could feel something traveling between us, something in the living room. *No*, she said. *But he was there.*

When I got home and told my mom about the dream, she said my grandma sometimes said these things, and that she got ideas from stories. Story or not, the way my grandma told me was unrehearsed. She came out with it so simply and suddenly. He was there with her. Forget skepticism, and forget the half-hearted acknowledgment of both sides. If you don't believe in ghosts, you don't believe in your own interstices. More lives in us than we can know.

○

Or: More lives in us than we can know, but we are better at feeling than at knowing. One month after I returned to Denver, I visited the gastroenterologist's office to give a routine sample of blood. The physician's assistant failed to find my vein. He poked me a second time but did not fill every vial. He said the vein had given everything it had. He was going to have to return to my other arm.

While I clenched my fist to bring the veins up, I saw a bead of blood blooming from the mark of the first needle. I felt my vision going. Like that, I was gone. I woke up in his arms, being dragged to an examination room. I was covered in sweat. The seat of my pants felt wet too, and slowly I became aware of the smell.

In the examination room, a haunting gathered around me. The PA talked nervously. He told me I was gray and green. The office manager came in. Two nurses arrived. They asked me if I wanted animal crackers or Starburst. How about apple juice? More and more I smelled what came off me, and I tried to ignore it. They brought me the juice. The office manager sent out the nervous PA. She apologized. I knew, but I wouldn't let myself understand, that she was apologizing for her own and everyone else's presence at a moment she knew would be unforgettably embarrassing for me.

I couldn't reach Thirii, so I drove home trying not to look at my pants. I walked up the stairs of our apartment building slowly. When I entered, she stood at the door. I couldn't make eye contact. I went into the shower and stripped. I washed the shit off my underwear and pants. I threw them in a wad on the floor of the tub and stood there for a long time, not moving, staring at the shower curtain.

Later I threw out my underwear. My pants, Thirii washed by hand. She did it matter of factly, drizzling them with detergent and wringing them over the drain. The smell slowly dissipated, even though I kept catching hints of it the rest of the night. Before we went to bed, I asked her to take care of me. I didn't have anything left in me. I needed her to understand that I was not all right.

The next day she did everything. She made breakfast, did dishes, went out to get us lunch. After we ate I sat against her on the bed. While she brushed my hair, I brought out my phone to interview her. Like I had asked my parents, I asked her: Do you believe in ghosts? I still felt haunted. I wanted to capture my ghost, to name it. I wanted to understand what was in me, and what had been in us.

There were some things she said that I had heard her say before. There was the Theravada Buddhist cosmology, which consists of 31 planes of existence. Because, like us, they live in the bottom five planes, demons and hungry ghosts sometimes travel through the human realm. There was also pre-Buddhist Burmese animism, in which every thing and being has a spirit. Then Thirii said something I hadn't heard her say:

I used to think I did not have any powers, because I can't see things and I don't have prophetic dreams. But I think I do have some intuition, because I feel like I can feel things, even if I can't see or hear them.

I think some people can see or hear things, and it's more clear to them. But I definitely have feelings, and it's less clear because—only because feelings are less verifiable.

I think all my experience of ghosts has been like that. I'll feel scared of a place for no reason, and a desire to get away from it for no reason, and then I'll learn after the fact that maybe there was a ghost there.

I asked her whether she thought ghosts had affected our relationship. There was a pause, and she started laughing, and I started laughing. Maybe the question was absurd. But she became serious again. She said:

I don't think I've ever even told you this. But I think that sometimes we can be ghosts to ourselves. Or there's parts of us that can inhabit us or possess us that maybe we don't fully identify with. So for example, I think when someone gets angry they're being inhabited by a ghost. But it's not like an outside ghost. It's just the ghost inside of you. You become somebody else. You become not yourself.

I sometimes almost feel like my spirit is not getting along with your spirit because one or both of us is contaminated by something.

Do you think there's a way to not let those ghosts get ahold of us?

Yeah, I think so.

I think ghosts fill empty spaces. And so I think that when I feel angry, it's because there's a space for that anger being created inside of me. Because I'm not actually acknowledging how I feel, which could take up that space instead. I think I get possessed by that feeling because I'm not allowing myself to feel the feeling that's actually there.

Say I feel sad. If I don't allow myself to feel sad, there's an emptiness where the sadness could have been. So the anger rushes in to fill it.

I think that's why my solution to feeling bad is to actually allow myself to feel bad, rather than push it away.

Yeah. Because the ghosts can't get in?

Also, well, because the feeling of feeling bad—whatever you're feeling, anger, guilt—is never as bad as the empty space that you create instead.

I don't think the ghost is bad. I just think it's fake. It's shallow, or hollow, or something. It's just a distraction.

But it can be bad, I think. If that starts becoming you. If it lives in you long enough.

Soon, as had happened with my mom and my dad, the conversation felt too intimate to keep recording. I pressed the stop button and we just talked. My scalp grew warm as she ran the brush over it and down my neck. Like my visits to my grandma, some things must remain unwritten. Sometimes it is writing that gives birth to a ghost.

That day, I was too sick to leave the house. I stayed inside because I was embarrassed, because I was too depleted to carry myself into the world, but also because there was a magnetic power to the walls we slept inside. Recently we had decided to begin buying bottled water, based on the age of our building. We worried that we had been ingesting lead all this time. We wanted badly to identify the thing we felt inhabiting our house, but of course there was more to it than the water.

There was the early summer afternoon, which lent a calm light to the bedroom.

There were the leaves quaking outside.

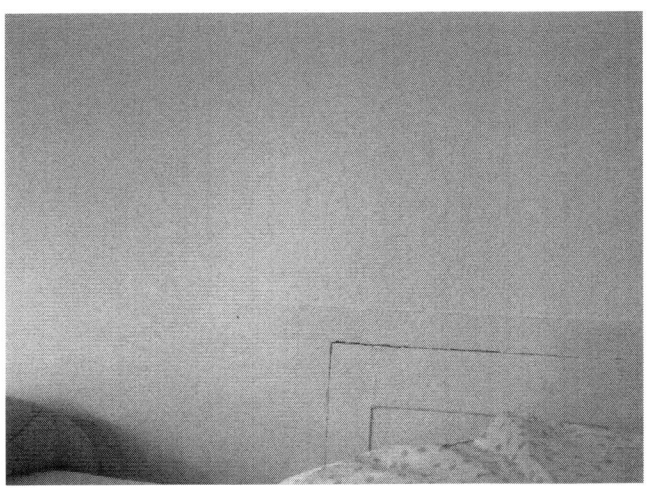

There was the still fan overhead, and the colorlessness of everything.

At moments like this, our home felt as if it had emptied out.

At moments like this, ghosts lived here only insofar as they were us. We haunted the house. Our gaps and spaces inhabited us. The only thing we could do was stop trying to chase away our ghosts and started trying to feel.

Funny—I wrote *heal* the first time I tried to type that last word. It sounded the same, like part of me was coming to life.

DENNIS JAMES SWEENEY's fiction, nonfiction, and poetry have appeared in *Crazyhorse*, *Five Points*, *Ninth Letter*, *The New York Times*, and *The Southern Review*, among others. He is a Small Press Editor of *Entropy*, the recipient of an MFA from Oregon State University, and a former Fulbright fellow in Malta. Originally from Cincinnati, he lives in Amherst, Massachusetts, where he is completing a PhD in Creative Writing at the University of Denver. He is the author of three previous chapbooks: *Poems About Moss*, *THREATS*, and *What They Took Away*.